About the Author

Mr. Paul Watson has many years of experience in working with BDD and Cucumber. He has worked on large software projects in USA, UK, Singapore, Hong Kong, Dubai, Australia and Switzerland.

His hobbies include travelling to new tourist places, watching basketball, cricket, Soccer and learning latest technological stuff.

Who is this book for

This book is for software developers, automation testers, Devops and engineers working on IT project. Whether you are a beginner or an experienced developer, this book will help you master the skills on Cucumber.

The book starts with introduction of Cucumber and then dives into key concepts like creating project in IntelliJ IDEA, using tags, plugins, integration with Junit, executing selenium tests, using picocontainer and lamda expressions.

Preface

This book is for those who are new to Cucumber. It will help you understand what is Cucumber and how you can use it in your software project.

In this book, you will learn below topics.

1. Introduction to Cucumber
2. Installation of Cucumber
3. Writing feature files using Gherkin
4. Adding Cucumber dependency to Java project
5. Cucumber Test
6. Executing Cucumber tests using Cucumber class
7. Cucumber options
8. Filtering scenarios
9. Passing parameters to steps
10. Passing the data table to steps
11. Feature file variations
12. Running multiple feature files in Cucumber
13. Sharing selenium Webdriver instance using PicoContainer
14. Reports in Cucumber
15. Cucumber using Lambda Expressions

1. Introduction

Cucumber is the BDD (Behavior driven development) testing framework.

Key things to note about Cucumber are -

1. Open source BDD testing framework.
2. Cross platform framework.
3. Tests are written in various languages like English, French, German and many more using Gherkin Syntax.
4. We can write the tests in various programming languages like Ruby, JRuby, PHP, Java, Jython, Groovy, Javascript, Clojure, Gosu, Lua, .Net, PHP, C++ and TCL
5. Integrates very well with CI servers like Jenkins and TeamCity
6. Reports can be generated in HTML, JSON, JUnit style
7. Capybara - the testing framework - is a part of Cucumber
8. Integrates very well with frameworks like Selenium, Appium, Spring, Watir, Ruby on Rails etc.

2. Installation of Cucumber

Setting up Cucumber is very simple.

You will need to install below tools.

1. Java JDK
2. Java IDE - IntelliJ IDEA or Eclipse
3. Cucumber library
4. Build tools like Maven or gradle
5. IntelliJ IDEA Plugins - Gherkin and cucumber for Java

Below image shows the IntelliJ plugins that you need.

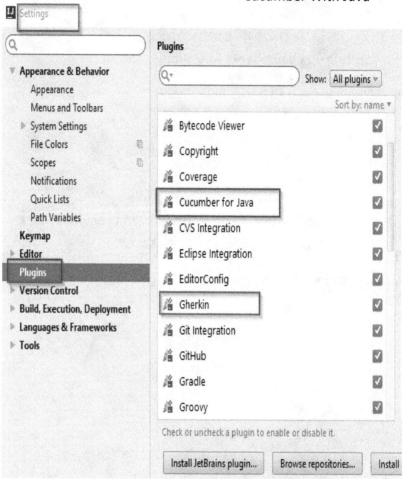

Cucumber and Gherkin plugins in IntelliJ IDEA

Create a simple Maven or gradle project and add below dependency.

```xml
<dependency>

    <groupId>info.cukes</groupId>

    <artifactId>cucumber-java</artifactId>

    <version>1.2.4</version>

    <scope>test</scope>

</dependency>
```

For writing the test steps using lambda expression in Java 8, you will have to add below dependency.

```xml
<dependency>

    <groupId>info.cukes</groupId>

    <artifactId>cucumber-java8</artifactId>

    <version>1.2.4</version>

    <scope>test</scope>

</dependency>
```

You also need below JUnit dependencies to integrate Cucumber with JUnit.

```
<dependency>

    <groupId>junit</groupId>

    <artifactId>junit</artifactId>

    <version>4.12</version>

    <scope>test</scope>

</dependency>


<dependency>

    <groupId>info.cukes</groupId>

    <artifactId>cucumber-junit</artifactId>

    <version>1.2.4</version>

    <scope>test</scope>

</dependency>
```

3. Writing feature files using Gherkin

BDD is an emerging software development model used along with agile methodologies.

Some of the key things to know about BDD are -

1. Dan North created first BDD framework - Jbehave
2. Other BDD frameworks are Rbehave, Rspec, Cucumber, Behat
3. The tests are written in plain text in the form of stories or features
4. The Domain specific language (Gherkin) is used for writing the tests.

What is Gherkin?

Gherkin is the plain text language used to write feature files (also called as story files) in BDD frameworks like cucumber. Gherkin is implemented in most of languages in the world like English, German, French....many more. This means that any project stakeholder can write, read and understand the tests written in Gherkin. That's the crux of the Gherkin language.

Key points to note about feature file

1. Each feature file can contain one or more scenarios and optinally outline and background.
2. Each scenario has steps like given, when, and, then, but

What are the keywords in Gherkin?

Gherkin has reserved some keywords which have specific meaning in the context of feature files.

Below is the list of keywords in Gherkin.

1. Given - used to specify the precondition of the scenario
2. When - used to specify the action
3. And - used to specify additional preconditions and actions
4. Then - used to specify the result of the action
5. Feature - Used to specify the description of the feature
6. Scenario - Used to specify the description of the scenario
7. Outline and Examples
8. Background - Used to specify the action to be taken before each scenario in the feature file is executed.
9. """ - used to pass data in multi-line format
10. | - used to pass data in table format
11. @ - used to tag scenarios and features
12. # - used to comment the line in feature file

Below feature file will make you understand most of the syntax of Gherkin language.

Basic Sample feature file

Now let us take a look at simplest feature file that we can have in gherkin.

```
Feature: ATM Card authentication

  User should be asked for the PIN once ATM
card is inserted into the ATM machine.

    User should be given warning message if PIN
number entered is wrong.

User should be authenticated successfully if
PIN number entered is correct.


  Scenario: Enter wrong PIN at ATM

    Given I insert the ATM card in ATM machine

    And I am asked to enter the PIN

    When I enter the correct PIN

    Then I should be able to see option to
withdraw money
```

Sample feature file with Outline and Examples keyword

Scenario outline are used in cases where we need to repeat same set of actions but with different combination of data. For instance, In below scenario outline, we need to test the login functionality with different combinations of user id and password. In such cases, we use <VariableData> syntax to specify the varying data and it is supplied through examples keyword. So in below scenario, all steps will be executed 4 times - one for each user.

```
Scenario Outline: Password rules

  Given that we are on login page

  When we enter user id <ID> and password
<PASSWORD>

  Then the login should be <OUTCOME>


  Examples:

    | ID       | PASSWORD | OUTCOME |

    |   Sagar|   128$9#  |     Fail|

    |   Amol |   98sjdg  |    PASS|

    |  Shaun  |   jslsh9  |    PASS|

    |    Ben  |   KON()%  |     FAIL|
```

Sample feature file with Background

Background keyword is used when we want to execute certain number of steps before each scenario. For example, suppose you want to clear browser cookies before execution of each scenario, then we can use background keyword with step to clear cookies.

Passing input data to the step

Each scenario can have multiple steps and each step is the user action. A step is like specific operation in the system. A steps may need the input data to be processed. We can pass the input to the step using 3 ways.

1. In-line Variables
2. Multi-line string
3. Tables

Grouping the scenarios and features with tags

We use tags to group similar scenarios and features together in Gherkin. @ symbol is used for tagging the scenarios and features.

4. Adding Cucumber dependency to Java project

To write the tests using cucumber, we need to add 2 types of dependencies.

1. cucumber-java
2. junit

If you are using Maven build management system, you can use below XML block in POM.XML

```
<dependency>

<groupId>info.cukes</groupId>

<artifactId>cucumber-java</artifactId>

<version>1.2.4</version>

</dependency>


<dependency>

    <groupId>junit</groupId>

    <artifactId>junit</artifactId>

    <version>4.12</version>

    <scope>test</scope>

</dependency>
```

5. Cucumber Test

5.1 Writing first cucumber test

Just follow below steps to write first cucumber test in IntelliJ IDEA.

1. Create a maven project.
2. Add feature file containing scenarios in Test Resources directory.
3. Add the maven dependency for Cucumber.
4. Write step definitions and execute the tests from feature file.

Here is the feature file that we created and put in the test resources folder.

```
@selenium

Feature: My feature


  Scenario: Verify title

    Given I am on the www.softpost.org home
page

    Then I verify that title contains tutorials
```

Note that we have not added the step definitions for above steps in feature file. When you execute the feature file, you will see below errors.

You can implement missing steps with the snippets below:

```java
@Given("^I am on the www\\.softpost\\.org home
page$")
public void
i_am_on_the_www_softpost_org_home_page() throws
Throwable {
// Write code here that turns the phrase above
into concrete actions
throw new PendingException();
}


@Then("^I verify that title contains
tutorials$")
public void
i_verify_that_title_contains_tutorials() throws
Throwable {
// Write code here that turns the phrase above
into concrete actions
throw new PendingException();
}


Undefined step: Given I am on the
www.softpost.org home page

Undefined step: Then I verify that title
contains tutorials
```

Writing the step definitions

You can copy above method snippets and write your own code inside it. Alternatively, if you have cucumber for Java and Gherkin plugin installed in IntelliJ IDEA, then you can create the step definitions by pressing alt + enter on the steps in Feature file as shown in below image.

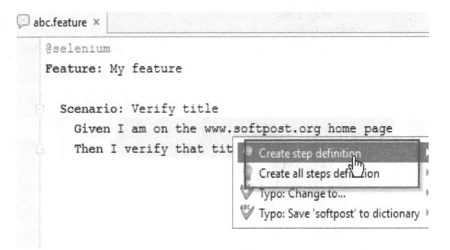

Creating cucumber step definitions in IntelliJ IDEA

Here is the class with step definitions.

```
package org.softpost;
import cucumber.api.java.After;
import cucumber.api.java.Before;
import cucumber.api.java.en.Given;
import cucumber.api.java.en.Then;
import junit.framework.Assert;
import org.openqa.selenium.WebDriver;
import
org.openqa.selenium.firefox.FirefoxDriver;
/**
 * Created by Sagar on 12-07-2016.
 */
```

```
@SuppressWarnings("ALL")
public class seleniumsteps
    {
    WebDriver driver;
    @Before
    public void launchBrowser(){
        driver = new FirefoxDriver();
    }
    @Given("^I am on the www\\.softpost\\.org
home page$")
    public void
i_am_on_the_www_softpost_org_home_page() throws
Throwable
{
        driver.get("http://www.softpost.org");
    }
    @Then("^I verify that title contains
tutorials$")
    public void
i_verify_that_title_contains_tutorials() throws
Throwable
    {

Assert.assertTrue(driver.getTitle().toLowerCase
().contains("tutorials"));
    }
    @After
    public void killBrowser()
{
        driver.close();
        driver.quit();
    }
}
```

After writing the step definitions, you can create the run configuration for feature file as shown in below image. Note that Glue property is very important. You should specify the package name that contains step definitions in the Glue.

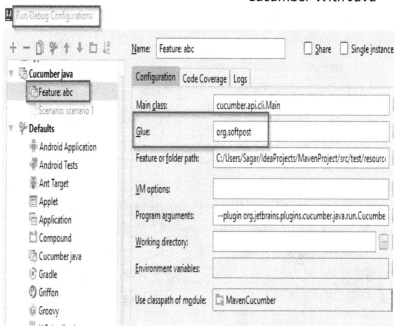

glue in Cucumber run configuration

Then you can right click on feature file and run the test as shown in below image.

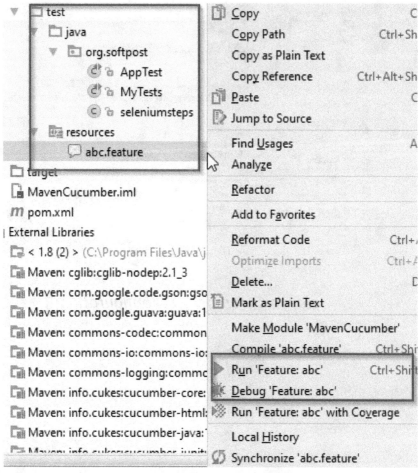

Running cucumber feature file in IntelliJ IDEA

If everything is ok, tests will run successfully.

Cucumber Reports in IntelliJ IDEA

You can view report of execution as shown in below images.

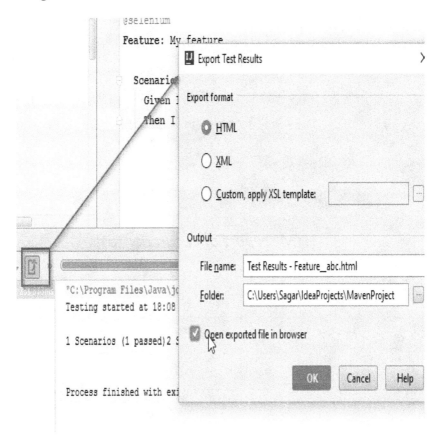

Viewing cucumber execution report in IntelliJ IDEA

Feature: abc: 2 total, 2 passed
23.37 s

Collapse | Expand

Feature: My feature 23.37 s

Scenario: Verify title 23.37 s

Given I am on the www.softpost.org home page   passed   23.30 s

Then I verify that title contains tutorials   passed   75 ms

Generated by IntelliJ IDEA on 12/7/16 6:11 PM

HTML report of cucumber tests

6. Executing Cucumber tests using Cucumber class

To write the tests using JUnit @RunWith annotation, we need below dependencies.
cucumber.api.junit.Cucumber - This class is present in the cucumber-junit artifact library.

```
<dependency>

<groupId>junit</groupId>

<artifactId>junit</artifactId>

<version>4.12</version>

<scope>test</scope>

</dependency>


<dependency>

<groupId>info.cukes</groupId>

<artifactId>cucumber-junit</artifactId>

<version>1.2.4</version>

</dependency>
```

Then you can add below test class. After running the below test, cucumber generates the report at target/selenium-reports. Cucumber.class contains main method that reads the feature file and executes scenario in it.

```
package org.softpost;
import cucumber.api.CucumberOptions;
import cucumber.api.junit.Cucumber;
import org.junit.runner.RunWith;

@RunWith(Cucumber.class)
@CucumberOptions(
        features = "classpath:abc.feature",
        glue = "classpath:org.softpost",
        plugin = "html:target/selenium-reports"
)

public class MyTests
{
}
```

7. Cucumber options

When executing the cucumber scenarios, we can pass various options as mentioned below.

1. features - path of the features files
2. glue - path of the step definition classes
3. dry run - used to check that all step definitions are desinged
4. monochrome - true/false It controls the readability of the output
5. strict - false means that undefined steps are skipped. Test does not fail
6. name - used to filter the features and scenarios
7. plugin - json, html, junit, pretty
8. snippets - Snippet style can be Camel case or Underscore

Here is the sample test class showing all these options.

```
package org.softpost;
import cucumber.api.CucumberOptions;
import cucumber.api.SnippetType;
import cucumber.api.junit.Cucumber;
import org.junit.runner.RunWith;

@RunWith(Cucumber.class)
@CucumberOptions(
        features = "classpath:abc.feature",
        glue = "classpath:org.softpost",
        tags = "~@blocked",
        plugin = "html:target/selenium-
reports",
        dryRun = false,
        monochrome = true,
        strict = true,
        snippets = SnippetType.CAMELCASE
)

public class MyTests
{
}
```

8. Filtering scenarios

8.1 Tagging the scenarios

We can tag scenarios using @ symbol in Feature files as shown in below example. Note that we can also tag all the scenarios in a feature file by writing the tag at the beginning of the feature file. We can also associate multiple tags with the same scenario as well. In below example, we have tagged the scenario with 4 tags - selenium, regression, sanity and critical.

```
@selenium

Feature: My feature

    @regression @sanity @critical

    Scenario: Verify title

        Given I am on the www.softpost.org home
page

        Then I verify that title contains tutorials
```

To execute the scenarios with 2 tags say regression and critical, we can use below syntax.
tags = ["@regression","@critical"]

To execute the scenarios with 2 tags say regression or critical, we can use below syntax
tags = ["@regression,@critical"]

To skip the scenarios tagged with tag say sanity, we can use below syntax

Negative tags = ["~@sanity"]

We can also tie the @Before and @After methods with scenarios tagged with specific names.

For example, below before method will be executed only before the scenarios tagged with selenium

@Before("@selenium")

Here is the example showing the usage of tags in Cucumber.

Consider below feature file.

```
@selenium

Feature: My feature

    @regression @sanity @critical

    Scenario: Verify softpost title

    Given I am on the www.softpost.org home
page

    Then I verify that title contains tutorials

    @sanity

    Scenario: Verify yahoo title

        Given I am on the www.yahoo.com home
page
```

```
        Then I verify that title contains
tutorials
```

Now take a look at below Test Class. After executing below test class, only first scenario will be executed because that scenario is tagged with @sanity and @regression

```java
package org.softpost;
import cucumber.api.CucumberOptions;
import cucumber.api.SnippetType;
import cucumber.api.junit.Cucumber;
import org.junit.runner.RunWith;

@RunWith(Cucumber.class)
@CucumberOptions(
        features = "classpath:abc.feature",
        glue = "classpath:org.softpost",
        tags = {"@sanity","@regression"},
        plugin = "html:target/selenium-
reports",
        dryRun = false,
        monochrome = true,
        strict = true,
        snippets = SnippetType.CAMELCASE
)

public class MyTest
{
}
```

Now take a look at below test class. After executing below test, both scenarios will be executed as both are tagged with @sanity tag.

```
package org.softpost;
import cucumber.api.CucumberOptions;
import cucumber.api.SnippetType;
import cucumber.api.junit.Cucumber;
import org.junit.runner.RunWith;

@RunWith(Cucumber.class)
@CucumberOptions(
        features = "classpath:abc.feature",
        glue = "classpath:org.softpost",
        tags = {"@sanity,@regression"},
        plugin = "html:target/selenium-
reports",
        dryRun = false,
        monochrome = true,
        strict = true,
        snippets = SnippetType.CAMELCASE
)

public class MyTest
{
}
```

Now take a look at below test class. After executing below test class, none of the scenarios will be executed as tag is prefixed with ~.

```
package org.softpost;
import cucumber.api.CucumberOptions;
import cucumber.api.junit.Cucumber;
import org.junit.runner.RunWith;

@RunWith(Cucumber.class)
```

```
@CucumberOptions(
        features = "classpath:abc.feature",
        glue = "classpath:org.softpost",
        tags = {"~@sanity"},
        plugin = "html:target/selenium-reports"
)

public class MyTest
{
}
```

8.2 Using name option

We can execute the specific scenarios with their names matching typical pattern.

For example - Consider below feature file.

```
@selenium

Feature: My feature

    @regression @sanity @critical

    Scenario: Verify softpost title

        Given I am on the www.softpost.org
home page

        Then I verify that title contains
tutorials

    @sanity

    Scenario: Verify yahoo title

        Given I am on the www.yahoo.com
home page
```

> Then I verify that title contains
> tutorials

To execute only those scenarios with name containing "softpost", we can use below test class. Note that we can also use regular expression as well to specify the value of scenario name.

```
package org.softpost;
import cucumber.api.CucumberOptions;
import cucumber.api.junit.Cucumber;
import org.junit.runner.RunWith;

@RunWith(Cucumber.class)
@CucumberOptions(
        features = "classpath:abc.feature",
        glue = "classpath:org.softpost",
        name = {"softpost"},
        plugin = "html:target/selenium-reports"
)

public class MyTest
{
}
```

9. Passing parameters to steps

We can pass the parameters to the step methods from feature file as shown in below scenario. In below scenario, we have passed the name of website in Given step.

The main advantage of passing the parameters is that we can re-use same step method in different scenarios with different parameters.

```
@selenium

Feature: Simple feature


  Scenario: Test web title

    Given I am on "www.yahoo.com" page

    Then I verify that the title is "yahoo"


  Scenario: Test web title

    Given I am on "www.softpost.org" page

    Then I verify that the title is
"tutorials"
```

Here are the step definitions for above steps. Note that both scenarios re-use same step definitions with different parameters.

```java
package org.softpost;

import com.google.common.primitives.Bytes;
import cucumber.api.Scenario;
import cucumber.api.java.After;
import cucumber.api.java.Before;
import cucumber.api.java.en.Given;
import cucumber.api.java.en.Then;
import junit.framework.Assert;
import org.openqa.selenium.OutputType;
import org.openqa.selenium.TakesScreenshot;
import org.openqa.selenium.WebDriver;
import
org.openqa.selenium.firefox.FirefoxDriver;


public class seleniumsteps
{
    WebDriver driver;
    Scenario scenario;

    @Before("@selenium")
    public void launchBrowser(Scenario
scenario)
    {
        driver = new FirefoxDriver();
        this.scenario = scenario;
        System.out.println("Executing scenario
" + scenario.getName());
    }

    @After("@selenium")
    public void killBrowser()
    {
        scenario.write("Finished scenario");
        if (scenario.isFailed())
        {
scenario.embed(((TakesScreenshot)driver).getScr
eenshotAs(OutputType.BYTES), "image/png");
```

```
        }
        driver.close();
        driver.quit();
    }


    @Given("^I am on \"([^\"]*)\" page$")
    public void i_am_on_page(String arg1)
throws Throwable
    {
        driver.get("http://" + arg1);
    }


    @Then("^I verify that the title is
\"([^\"]*)\"$")
    public void
i_verify_that_the_title_is(String arg1) throws
Throwable
    {

Assert.assertTrue(driver.getTitle().toLowerCase
().contains(arg1));

    }
}
```

10. Passing the data table to steps

10.1 Key - Value pair Datatable

We can pass the Data table with key and value as shown in below example.

```
Feature: Simple Datatable feature

  Scenario: Test web title

    Given I am on home page of xyz site

    And I submit the form with below details

      |name      | sagar  |

      |id        | 98989  |

      |address   | mumbai |

    Then I see that form submission is
successful
```

Here is the step definition class for above scenario. Note how we have converted the data table to map and accessed the keys and values.

```
package org.softpost;

import cucumber.api.DataTable;
import cucumber.api.java.en.Given;
import cucumber.api.java.en.Then;
import java.util.List;
import java.util.Map;

/**
 * Created by Sagar on 13-07-2016.
```

```
*/
public class DatatableSteps
{


    @Given("^I am on home page of xyz site$")
    public void i_am_on_home_page_of_xyz_site()
throws Throwable
    {
        System.out.println("Navigate to home
page \n");
    }

    @Given("^I submit the form with below
details$")
    public void
i_submit_the_form_with_below_details(DataTable
arg1) throws Throwable
    {
        Map<String,String> m =
arg1.asMap(String.class,String.class);
        System.out.println("\nFilling form with
below data\n");
        for( String k : m.keySet())
        {
            System.out.println("Key -> " + k +
" Value -> " + m.get(k));
        }
    }

    @Then("^I see that form submission is
successful$")
    public void
i_see_that_form_submission_is_successful()
throws Throwable
{
        System.out.println("\nVerify form
success message");
    }
}
```

Here is the output of execution of above feature file.

Navigate to home page

Filling form with below data

```
Key -> name Value -> sagar
Key -> id Value -> 98989
Key -> address Value -> mumbai

Verify form success message
1 Scenarios (1 passed)
3 Steps (3 passed)
0m0.525s
```

10.2 Multiple column datatable in Cucumber

Now let us look at how to pass the data table with multiple columns in Cucumber.

```
Feature: Multiple column data table

  Scenario: Create new student records

  Given We have below list of students
    | name      | id      | address  |
    | sagar     | 288345  |Brisbane  |
    | watson    | 38829   | London   |
    | paul      | 34223   |Chicago   |
```

Now take a look at below Student Class. This class is mapped with the data table.

```java
package org.softpost;

/**
 * Created by Sagar on 13-07-2016.
 */
public class Student
{
    private String name;
    private String address;
    private int id;

    public Student(String name, int id, String
address)
    {
        this.name = name;
        this.id = id;
        this.address = address;
    }

    public void printStudent()
    {
        System.out.println("\nStudent -> " + name
+", " + id + ", " + address);
    }
}
```

Now look at the step definition class. Note how we have converted the Data table to the list of student objects.

```java
package org.softpost;

import cucumber.api.DataTable;
import cucumber.api.java.en.Given;
import cucumber.api.java.en.Then;

import java.util.List;
import java.util.Map;
```

```
/**
 * Created by Sagar on 13-07-2016.
 */
public class DatatableSteps
{

    @Given("^We have below list of students$")
    public void
we_have_below_list_of_students(DataTable arg1)
throws Throwable
    {
        List<Student> students =
arg1.asList(Student.class);

        for(Student s : students)
        {
            s.printStudent();
        }
    }
}
```

Here is the output of above code.

```
Testing started at 19:48 ...


Student -> sagar, 288345, Brisbane


Student -> watson, 38829, London


Student -> paul, 34223, Chicago
1 Scenarios (1 passed)
1 Steps (1 passed)
0m0.635s
```

11. Feature file variations

11.1 Scenario Background

Sometimes, we need to execute certain steps, before every scenario in the same feature file. Backgrounds allow you to reuse same steps across multiple scenarios.
For example - to test some feature, we might need to filter records before every scenario. So we can put the steps required to filter the records inside
Background. These steps would be executed every time each scenario in the same feature file is executed.

In below feature file, we have one step in the background (Given I filter some records). This step will be executed before every scenario in this feature file.

```
Feature: Simple background feature

  Background: Execute before every scenario

    Given I filter some records

  Scenario: Verify delete functionality

    Given I click on the delete button of
the first record

    Then I verify that record is removed
from the table

  Scenario: Verify Update functionality
```

> Given I click on update button of the first record
>
> Then I verify that record opens in new window and we can modify it

Here is the step definition class.

```java
package org.softpost;

import cucumber.api.java.en.Given;
import cucumber.api.java.en.Then;

/**
 * Created by Sagar on 13-07-2016.
 */
public class backgroundsteps {


    @Given("^I filter some records$")
    public void i_filter_some_records() throws
Throwable {
        System.out.println("\n\nBackground -
Filtering some records\n");
    }

    @Given("^I click on the delete button of
the first record$")
    public void
i_click_on_the_delete_button_of_the_first_recor
d() throws Throwable {
        System.out.println("Click delete
button\n");
    }

    @Then("^I verify that record is removed
from the table$")
```

```
    public void
i_verify_that_record_is_removed_from_the_table(
) throws Throwable {
        System.out.println("Verify deleted
record\n");
    }


    @Given("^I click on update button of the
first record$")
    public void
i_click_on_update_button_of_the_first_record()
throws Throwable {
        System.out.println("Click update
button\n");
    }


    @Then("^I verify that record opens in new
window and we can modify it$")
    public void
i_verify_that_record_opens_in_new_window_and_we
_can_modify_it() throws Throwable {
        System.out.println("Verify modified
record\n");
    }


}
```

Here is the output of execution of above feature file.

Background - Filtering some records
Click delete button
Verify deleted record

Background - Filtering some records
Click update button
Verify modified record

2 Scenarios (2 passed)

6 Steps (6 passed)

0m0.578s

11.2 Scenario outline

Sometimes, we need to execute the same scenario but with different test data. In such cases, we can use the concept called as scenario outline. In below example, same scenario will be executed twice. First time with 99 and 100. Second time with 11 and 200.

```
Feature: Outline feature

  Scenario Outline: Addition of numbers

    When I add integers <i1> and <i2>

    Then I see the result as <sum>

    Examples:

      | i1     | i2    | sum     |

      |     99 | 100   |     199 |

      |     11 | 200   |     211 |
```

Here is the step definitions class.

```
package org.softpost;

import cucumber.api.java.en.Then;
import cucumber.api.java.en.When;
import junit.framework.Assert;
```

```
/**
 * Created by Sagar on 13-07-2016.
 */
public class outlinesteps
{
    int result = 0;
    @When("^I add integers (\\d+) and (\\d+)$")
    public void i_add_integers_and(int arg1,
int arg2) throws Throwable
    {
      result = arg1 + arg2;
        System.out.println("Adding " + arg1 + "
and " + arg2 + "\n\n");
    }

    @Then("^I see the result as (\\d+)$")
    public void i_see_the_result_as(int arg1)
throws Throwable
    {
        Assert.assertEquals(result,arg1);
    }

}
```

Here is the output of execution of above feature file.

Testing started at 19:18 ...
Adding 99 and 100

Adding 11 and 200

2 Scenarios (2 passed)
4 Steps (4 passed)
0m0.595s

12. Running multiple feature files in Cucumber

We can execute scenarios in multiple feature files as shown in below example. We are running 2 feature files - multicolumn and outline. Note that to execute all feature files, we can also use * operator.

```
package org.softpost;
import cucumber.api.CucumberOptions;
import cucumber.api.junit.Cucumber;
import org.junit.runner.RunWith;

@RunWith(Cucumber.class)
@CucumberOptions(
        features =
{"classpath:multicolumn.feature","classpath:out
line.feature"},
        glue = "classpath:org.softpost",
        plugin = "html:target/selenium-reports"
)

public class MultipleFeatureTest
{
}
```

Here is the HTML report generated after execution of above test class.

▼ **Feature**: Multiple column data table
  ▼ **Scenario**: Create new student records
    Given We have below list of students

name	id	address
sagar	288345	Brisbane
watson	38829	London
paul	34223	Chicago

▼ **Feature**: Outline feature
  ▶ **Scenario Outline**: Addition of numbers
  ▶ **Scenario Outline**: Addition of numbers
  ▶ **Scenario Outline**: Addition of numbers

Multiple feature files in Cucumber

13. Sharing selenium Webdriver instance using PicoContainer

In Selenium automation, we create a WebDriver instance. But we can not use the same driver instance in different step definition classes in Cucumber.

We can share the same Webdriver instance in 2 ways.

1. By creating a static Webdriver
2. By using PicoContainer (Dependency Injection)

First method is very simple. Just create a class with Static WebDriver field.

Now let us take a look at how we can share the same driver using Dependency Injection. For this, you will need below dependencies.

```
<dependency>

<groupId>org.seleniumhq.selenium</groupId>

        <artifactId>selenium-
java</artifactId>

        <version>2.42.2</version>

</dependency>
```

```
<dependency>

        <groupId>info.cukes</groupId>

        <artifactId>cucumber-
picocontainer</artifactId>

        <version>1.2.4</version>

        <scope>test</scope>

</dependency>
```

Next, we need to create a class where we will create a Webdriver instance as shown in below example. Note that we instantiates the driver only once. We have got a method getDriver to get the driver.

```java
package org.softpost;

import cucumber.api.java.After;
import cucumber.api.java.Before;
import org.openqa.selenium.WebDriver;
import
org.openqa.selenium.firefox.FirefoxDriver;

public class SharedClass
{

    private static boolean startBrowser =
false;

    private WebDriver driver;
    public String title = "";

    @Before("@sharedselenium")
    public void init() throws Exception
    {
```

```
        if (!startBrowser)
        {

            driver = new FirefoxDriver();

                //To stop launching browser after
every scenario, assign below variable with true
value
                startBrowser = false;
        }
    }

    public WebDriver getDriver()
    {
        return driver;
    }

    @After("@sharedselenium")
    public void cleanUp()
    {
        driver.close();
        driver.quit();

    }
}
```

Next in the step definition classes, we can pass the instance of above class as shown in below example. Note that we are using getDriver() method to access the driver instance. So similarly you can pass the instance of SharedClass to any step definition class that wants to use the driver. PicoContainer is used internally to wire up dependent classes.

```
package org.softpost;

import cucumber.api.java.en.Given;
import cucumber.api.java.en.Then;
import junit.framework.Assert;

public class ShareSeleniumSteps
{

    SharedClass sharedClass;

    public ShareSeleniumSteps(SharedClass
sharedClass)
    {
        this.sharedClass = sharedClass;
    }

    @Given("^I am on the www\\.softpost\\.org
home page$")
    public void
i_am_on_the_www_softpost_org_home_page() throws
Throwable
    {

sharedClass.getDriver().get("http://www.softpos
t.org");

    }

    @Then("^I verify that title contains
tutorials$")
    public void
i_verify_that_title_contains_tutorials() throws
Throwable
    {
        Assert.assertTrue(
sharedClass.getDriver().getTitle().toLowerCase(
).contains("tutorials"));
```

```
    }

    @Then("^I verify that title contains
tutooorials$")
    public void
i_verify_that_title_contains_tutooorials()
throws Throwable
    {
        Assert.assertTrue(
sharedClass.getDriver().getTitle().toLowerCase(
).contains("tutooorials"));
    }

}
```

14. Reports in Cucumber

14.1 Embedding the screenshot

When working in a selenium automation project, we often need to take a screenshot on test failure. Selenium API provides a way to take screenshot with the help of takesScreenshot interface.

Cucumber allows you to embed that screenshot in the Cucumber reports.

Here is the simple code.

```
@After("@selenium")
    public void killBrowser(Scenario scenario)
    {
        if (scenario.isFailed())
        {

scenario.embed(((TakesScreenshot)driver).getScr
eenshotAs(OutputType.BYTES), "image/png");
        }
        driver.close();
        driver.quit();
    }
```

Below image shows where to find the HTML report in Maven project.

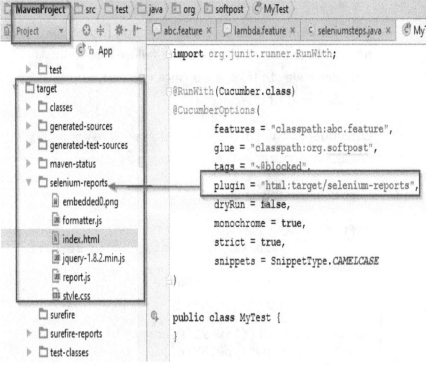

Cucumber report location in Maven project

Here is the sample HTML report showing the captured screenshot.

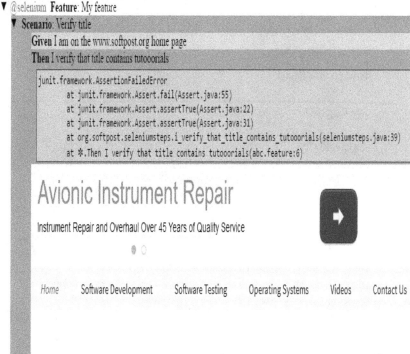

▼ @selenium **Feature**: My feature
  ▼ **Scenario**: Verify title
    Given I am on the www.softpost.org home page
    Then I verify that title contains tutooorials

```
junit.framework.AssertionFailedError
        at junit.framework.Assert.fail(Assert.java:55)
        at junit.framework.Assert.assertTrue(Assert.java:22)
        at junit.framework.Assert.assertTrue(Assert.java:31)
        at org.softpost.seleniumsteps.i_verify_that_title_contains_tutooorials(seleniumsteps.java:39)
        at *.Then I verify that title contains tutooorials(abc.feature:6)
```

Avionic Instrument Repair

Instrument Repair and Overhaul Over 45 Years of Quality Service

Home   Software Development   Software Testing   Operating Systems   Videos   Contact Us

Free software tutorials

Welcome to Softpost

Embeding the screenshot in Cucumber report

14.2 Writing to Cucumber HTML reports

We can write to Cucumber HTML report using write method of Scenario class.

Below step definition class illustrates how to write to HTML report. Note how we have passed scenario object to Before method.

```java
package org.softpost;

import com.google.common.primitives.Bytes;
import cucumber.api.Scenario;
import cucumber.api.java.After;
import cucumber.api.java.Before;
import cucumber.api.java.en.Given;
import cucumber.api.java.en.Then;
import junit.framework.Assert;
import org.openqa.selenium.OutputType;
import org.openqa.selenium.TakesScreenshot;
import org.openqa.selenium.WebDriver;
import org.openqa.selenium.firefox.FirefoxDriver;

/**
 * Created by Sagar on 12-07-2016.
 */
@SuppressWarnings("ALL")
public class seleniumsteps
{
    WebDriver driver;
    Scenario scenario;

    @Before("@selenium")
    public void launchBrowser(Scenario scenario)
    {
        driver = new FirefoxDriver();
        this.scenario = scenario;
    }
```

```
    @Given("^I am on the www\\.softpost\\.org
home page$")
    public void
i_am_on_the_www_softpost_org_home_page() throws
Throwable
    {
        driver.get("http://www.softpost.org");
        scenario.write("Navigated to
www.softpost.org");
    }

    @Then("^I verify that title contains
tutorials$")
    public void
i_verify_that_title_contains_tutorials() throws
Throwable
    {

Assert.assertTrue(driver.getTitle().toLowerCase
().contains("tutorials"));
    }

    @Then("^I verify that title contains
tutooorials$")
    public void
i_verify_that_title_contains_tutooorials()
throws Throwable
    {

Assert.assertTrue(driver.getTitle().toLowerCase
().contains("tutooorials"));
    }

    @After("@selenium")
    public void killBrowser()
      {
        scenario.write("Finished scenario");
        if (scenario.isFailed())
          {
```

```
scenario.embed(((TakesScreenshot)driver).getScr
eenshotAs(OutputType.BYTES), "image/png");
        }
        driver.close();
        driver.quit();
    }
}
```

Here is the sample HTML report.

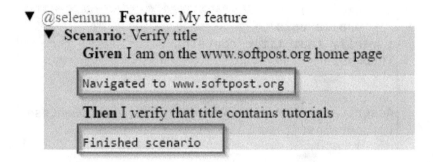

Writing to cucumber HTML report

15. Cucumber using Lambda Expressions

15.1 Cucumber dependency for using Lambda expressions in Java 8

In Java 8, Lambda expressions were introduced. Cucumber allows you to write step definitions using Lambda expressions.

You need to add below dependency to write tests using Lambda expressions.

```
<dependency>

        <groupId>info.cukes</groupId>

        <artifactId>cucumber-
java8</artifactId>

        <version>1.2.4</version>

        <scope>test</scope>

</dependency>
```

Ensure that JDK version is 1.8.0_51. Otherwise you will get below error.

Exception in thread "main" cucumber.runtime.CucumberException: Failed to instantiate class ....CucumberException: java.lang.IllegalArgumentException: Wrong type at constant pool index

15.2 Cucumber test using Lambda expressions

Now let us write sample cucumber step definitions using Lambda expressions.

Here is the sample feature file.

```
Feature: Lambda feature

  Scenario: Verify sum

    Given I add 1 and 2

    Then I verify that sum is 3
```

Here is the sample Test Class using Lambda expressions to write the step definitions. Note that StepClass must implement cucmber.api.java8.En interface and step methods should be inside the constructor of test class. You also need to ensure that Java language level should be 1.8.

```
package org.softpost;

import cucumber.api.java8.En;

public class StepClass8 implements En
{
    public StepClass8()
    {
        Given("^I add 1 and 2$", () -> {
            System.out.println("Adding 1 and
2");
        });

        Then("^I verify that sum is 3$", () ->
{
            System.out.println("Checking that
sum is 3");
```

```
        });
    }
}
```

If you are using Maven, you can specify the Java language level using below XML section in POM.XML

```xml
<build>

        <plugins>

            <plugin>

<groupId>org.apache.maven.plugins</groupId>

                <artifactId>maven-compiler-
plugin</artifactId>

                <version>2.3.2</version>

                <configuration>

                    <source>1.8</source>

                    <target>1.8</target>

                    <encoding>UTF-8</encoding>

                </configuration>

            </plugin>

        </plugins>

    </build>
```